Girl, Woman, Bird

poems by

Katherine Morgan

Finishing Line Press
Georgetown, Kentucky

Girl, Woman, Bird

Copyright © 2022 by Katherine Morgan
ISBN 978-1-64662-798-1 First Edition
All rights reserved under International and Pan-American Copyright Conventions. No part of this book may be reproduced in any manner whatsoever without written permission from the publisher, except in the case of brief quotations embodied in critical articles and reviews.

Publisher: Leah Huete de Maines

Editor: Christen Kincaid

Cover Art: Andrea LeBlanc

Author Photo: Beverly Conway

Cover Design: Elizabeth Maines McCleavy

Order online: www.finishinglinepress.com
also available on amazon.com

Author inquiries and mail orders:
Finishing Line Press
PO Box 1626
Georgetown, Kentucky 40324
USA

Table of Contents

Home, Circa 1964 1

Language of the Forgotten 2

The Pink Dress I 3

As if to Explain the World 4

A Tour of the Archives 5

An American Visits the Memorial
   For Twenty Thousand RAF Who Died 7

Monumental Inversion 8

Blackwater 9

Possibly the Coldest Day of the Year 10

Beasts in the Woods 11

Post Cards at the New York Historical Society 12

At the Mt. Plaisir Hotel 13

The Pink Dress II 14

What You Wanted 15

The Woman Confronts Her Nemesis 16

Walking to the Bus with My Mother 17

Elegy 18

For Emma 19

A Sharp-Shinned Hawk Holds Me 20

The Pink Dress III 21

Sometimes a White Sheet 22

Bird Woman 23

Birding the Boreal Forest 24

Notes 25

For Todd and Sarah

Home, Circa 1964

home. *n.* 1. *A house, apartment, or other shelter.* As in: where the heart is, or the correct place for a woman; where my mother will teach me how to make homemade bread, can homegrown plums, peaches, glittering gems in a jar. 2. *The location of one's domestic affections.* But no one tells me how to behave when my affections are non-domestic. They only say, "Be home by ten o'clock," and I want to know does it count if I'm sitting in the driveway in the blue Cadillac with my boyfriend, hands up my blouse, intent on getting to third base. He may reach home plate if we have enough time. Dad might appreciate the baseball analogy, but he flicks the porch light on and off, code for get inside, NOW. 3. *An institution.* May turn out to be St. Anne's Home for Unwed Mothers and I already have two friends who have made that trip. 4. **Related words**: *homesick.* adj. As in: My Dartmouth brother who is not homesick, writes me advice letters. What does *he* know? He's never been on a date in his life. 5. *homeschool* v. As in: being taught at home in the late stages of pregnancy; pay attention, Sis, keep your fingers on the home row; type as if your life depends on it: a-s-d-f space semi-l-k-j space; the lazy boy, the quick brown fox. 6. *hometown* n. As in: the place where the church congregation will wonder in whispers how such a nice girl from such a nice family went wrong.

Language of the Forgotten
after Titus Kaphar

The first time I see the installation it is as yet
        unlit. But I have read about it [know it]

Hewn out of a chunk of plantation oak, Tom's head
        and big ideas [liberty, equality, &c.] fill the space.

The head-shaped cavity urethaned   [to reflect light]
        I have to stand at an angle to see the full figure

of the African woman   [shoulders set, gaze steady]
        painted [or etched?] on the surface of the glass-front.

I pace back and forth [a stalker] cocking my head this way
        that way [angry]   [she disappears, comes back]

the essence of the enslaved black woman [silenced by
        the lack of light].

Another visit, I return for a second look. The LEDs are lit
        Behold!   [Good tidings]   She dominates

the inside of his profile,
        hands clasped at one hip   [defiant]

left elbow jabbed in the jut of his chin
        right elbow covering his wig at the tie-back

her apron skirt his cravat.
        His silhouette encircles her,   master

over her in life   [but not in art]
        In exchange for his body in her bed

she extracts a promise: freedom for [their] surviving children
        Beverly, Harriet, Madison, and Eston

The Pink Dress I

Wrapped in a clean sheet, all that remains
of my infant self: a handmade pink coat,
matching bonnet. Crinkled but silky,
the fabric reminds me of my mother's cool
hands on my feverish forehead,
the scent of her apple blossom cologne
and a hint of night air when she
came into my room to say good night.

I finger the smocking at the yoke,
smooth the delicate circles of featherstitch
on the Peter Pan collar, repeated along
the bonnet to frame my face. Tiny cuffs
turn back at the wrists. Years later,
we will repeat the delicate rose
for my first prom dress.
Measuring out yards of silk organza

my mother says, *the sky's the limit*
and on prom night,
she pins a few rosebuds, stems
wrapped in aluminum foil, to my dress,
ties a silver embroidered ribbon
around my waist as if to tether me
like a tame finch.

As if to Explain the World
after Bela Pratt, The Schoolboy of 1850

The figurine, imitation in plaster of Paris—
a parting gift—stands
at the back of my china cupboard,
dusty memento of an earlier life.

From the Latin *figura*, shape or form
language I never studied though my brothers
shouted *veni, vidi, vici* in the bedroom next to mine.
My mother would say: *Boys will be boys.*

The original bronze *Schoolboy of 1850*,
—a fine figure of a twelve-year-old
clad in straw hat, pants rolled below the knee,
right arm bent, apple clutched ready to eat—

was placed on a granite plinth in 1913,
at a coed school—to inspire the boys—
some of whom would wallow in trenches at Verdun,
their education in violence.

Days of Latin conjugations behind them,
they were figures on a ground of blood
and mud—this one will live, that one will die.
Could the *Schoolboy* be a trope for both genders

in the same way that *he* or *mankind*
erased half the human race in the texts I taught?
We girls aren't hungry, my mother would say
as she dished smaller portions for our plates.

A Tour of the Archives
at the Roger Tory Peterson Institute

Perched on a gunmetal cabinet, a Passenger Pigeon
    catches my eye. My guide asks,
        Would you like to see more bird skins?

Like a salesman displaying his wares,
    he slides open
        the shorebird drawer

where two Roseate Spoonbills—headless—touch,
    their legs tied in plié position,
        bent to fit their tomb.

Resting against a spoonbill's wing,
    a Glossy Ibis lies, feathers
        shimmer like heat waves

rising at the horizon: Bronze, green, faint rose.
    Saved separately, the predators,
        no longer terrorists of the skies,

peer from cotton-filled eye sockets.
    A Red-tailed Hawk cocks one wing
        as if to take flight.

The extinct inhabit their own vault:
    a Carolina Parakeet, green and yellow
        feathers so fresh

they could still decorate a woman's hat.
    At the back, an Ivory-billed Woodpecker
        wings bedraggled, beak in shadow

neck twisted. The last bird I saw,
       a Dusky Seaside Sparrow
              collected on Appledore Island

at the Isles of Shoals, 1877,
       where Celia Thaxter wrote poems,
              gardened, gathered artists to sketch.

They might have seen this very sparrow
       hopping in Celia's garden
              where I, too, have birded

and at the banding station have seen
       the mist nets alive with birds,
              felt their beating hearts.

An American Visits the Memorial for Twenty Thousand RAF Who Died
Runnymede, England, 2017

Panels line porticos, names chiseled
into stone, substitute graves for airmen

never found. Fake poppy wreaths, sit
beneath lists of the dead, blue cards

proclaim *Per Ardua ad Astra*,
through adversity to the stars.

One family honors their Uncle Fred
with his photo, a sprig of rosemary,

and a note: *With love
from nieces and nephews. (All 44 of us)*.

I opened the door to my grandparents' house
found them in tears, Grampa read aloud

in a hoarse voice, a letter in his trembling hand.
He dabbed his eyes with a handkerchief,

asked me to wait outside.
I retreated to the porch, gazed at the empty sky.

They read condolences written
after Uncle Dick, in his B-24, exploded

in flight from Reykjavik, on the way
to join these Englishmen, in battles not begun.

I look for his name, even though I know
I won't find it here.

Monumental Inversion
after Titus Kaphar

Incised in a slab of wood
then scorched,
shape of horse in mid-stride
[Washington the rider]   [no legs]
just hollow space, glass

blown into the silhouette
[horse only]   but wait
the head and neck broken away
[front leg missing]
misshapen vessels of glass litter

the foreground below—
[My rational mind]   [wants to imagine]
the sculpture back together
but floor-glass
was never horse

[the shapes are all wrong]
a deliberate deception.
[how do we understand
something that never was]
A disintegrating monument

to the realness of suffering.
General Washington, founding
father [slave owner]
Does the arc of history bend
[break]   toward justice

Blackwater
after Sally Mann

The reflection bleeds as the breeze
shuffles the water, and overhead
a cloud offers the only light,
enough to illuminate
the hopeless terrain
home to black bass,
catfish, blueback.
Not a bubble rises from muck,
layered with decades of leaves.

Over channels braided
by bald cypress roots, tupelo-lined
and tannin-stained,
trees shadow the still pools
where fugitive slaves once hid
under the silvered surface,
their bodies disappearing
into the dismal swamp.

Possibly the Coldest Day of the Year

Steam rose from the lake,
a pony wandered
under the willow tree,

or no, it was night in the cold woods, the dark sky,
well, dark except for the aurora
flashing like fireworks. Inside the house,

a bouquet of stargazer lilies
reeked a syrupy scent;
I longed to be outside

Frangipani's Bar, watching the muscled Adonis
grapple with the enormous blue lobster, heaving it
into the boat, using the gravity

that brought the iced willow branches crashing
to the ground, shattering the brittle snow
below. We were in the kitchen

when the first gunshot sounded, or no,
it was the crack and fall
of the first branch and we continued to argue

until the house shook,
the storm sheared limbs from the tree
and dropped them in a tangled web.

Beasts in the Woods

We hear men before we see
them, nearly ski into the deer

hung by the hind legs from a chain
strung across our would-be trail.

A bonfire sends sparks straight up,
snowmelt runs downslope.

Men in wool jackets, cap flaps
over their ears stand around, beer cans

in hand. Steam rises off the carcass,
the snow bloody below. One man

saws with a thin blade, ripping the velvet hide
from muscle with a sucking sound,

half the body naked. We skid to a stop,
kick up a spray of snow. Sudden silence.

We side step around the deer, avoid eye contact,
two women, hands sweaty in our gloves.

Post Cards at the New York Historical Society
    Without Sanctuary: Lynching Photography in America

I am in the room with these black
and white picture post cards—made
to share the lynching with faraway friends

or keep as a souvenir—sell
to a collector to frame and hang
and I am in the room, my heart

beats in my throat—each photo
depicts a new corpse—burned first,
whipped, naked, handcuffed.

I want to look away, but to do so seems
strange cowardice, some denial
these noosed men don't deserve.

My white face reflects in the glass,
a witness in the crowd.

At The Mt. Plaisir Hotel
Grande Rivière, Trinidad

The group leader gave the "halt" sign
hand raised above his head.
We hold flashlights red with Christmas bulbs—
white lights may cause the Leatherbacks
lumbering up from the high tideline
to turn back—create a circle of lights
around the female who labors
in the center her flippers digging
churning the sand, shoveling it to one side
then the other then turning her armored body
a few degrees to get a new angle for her toss.
Her six hundred pound body
sinks as she digs. The cavity
grows around this pre-historic female,
called to return to the place of her own hatching
the beach in front of the Mt. Plaisir Hotel.
As she settles into the chamber
the guide says "Feel free to touch
her head while she is in the egg-laying trance
she won't feel it." I recoil—the memory
of the delivery room, circle of people
hovering—Now, I want nothing more
than for the parents of the small boy
who is darting around the nest touching the head
of this laboring creature—to grab his hand
and make him stand still,
before I do.

The Pink Dress II
After Andrew Wyeth, Christina's World

Christina sprawls, back to the viewer,
propped on skeletal arms reaching
to the ground in front of her.
The artist says he saw her from his attic room.
She looks across a sea of browning hay,
to the house on the hill beyond, where he paints
hidden from her view. *She was coming back
from visiting the family grave, he says.*
Useless legs askew behind her,
she is like a killdeer feigning a wound,
ready to drag herself across the field.
He says he painted the field and the house first.
Her pale pink dress clings
to her torso broken by a narrow black belt.
She is perfect in her longing, her reaching.
He admits he posed his wife Betsy in the field.
Slanting light touches her shoulders,
outlines her hips in silver, illuminates
the limits of her world.
*He says he painted a memory,
more real than the thing itself.*

What You Wanted

A C-Scow on fire, your body
wrapped and lying on the hull, pushed
into Great Bay, to sail the Piscataqua
to the open ocean. Instead

a hillside Vermont cemetery,
cast assembled on frost-covered grass
in October air so sharp the depth of field
extends across the valley to the mountains.

You would crop this print, cut
the sisters, the brother, two ex-wives
— only the daughter would remain—
the photo dodged and burned to highlight

the tear fixed on her cheek,
the slight glitter of the granite gravestone,
sunlight focused on *Beloved brother, father, son,*
trinity of lies. An elderly woman at the edge

weeps at the gravestone of your brother,
a walk-on mourner in this circle of confusion.
A raven, fierce against a blue sky, flew at me
veered at the last moment.

The Woman Confronts Her Nemesis

Ink spreads on paper,
a Rorschach test,
who saw what in the dark swirls
the smoke of a thousand pages burning
waking the condors in the mountains
the conch shells in the ocean,
creamy white and pink
like a naked baby or a new mouse
dead in the nest.
One of us may have cried
eaten the rotten fruit between us.

The blot obliterates my words
raises questions
like the eyebrows
of a ninety-year-old man
dressed in a half-open kimono.
You sipped hibiscus tea
wrapped a rattlesnake around your wrist.
I have a jackknife, I will save you,
cut an X and suck the venom
or I could let you shrivel and die.
Who would I be without you?

Walking to the Bus With My Mother
Lillingston Canyon Road, Carpinteria, CA

Twirling in red plaid
lace-edged, creased
where you let down the hem,
I am dizzy
from spinning.
The lemon grove
backdrop for my dance
a green blur. When I stop,
my lunchbox bangs my leg,
the road uneasy
under my feet.

Braceros on ladders
lean against trees, drop
lemons into burlap sacks slung
like pocketbooks
across their chests,
whistle, clap and cat-call.
You grab my hand,
hustle toward the bus stop.
Dance over, I scuff
and crunch my shoes
through sunshine
on sycamore leaves.

Years later, I hold your hand
through your dark canyon pass,
and wonder, did they whistle
when you walked back
without me?

Elegy

Autumn blaze
gives way to thin   winter light
skins slip

as I plant
paper whites   in deep
reveal corms

smooth pearls.
Hands stiff,
I rise   gloves wet

from earth   ice-flecked.
My mother's hands
rest on sheets

white on white,
skin paper thin,
pearl in her ring   worn nub.

Blue veins
map years   layers
ready to slough

like narcissus   buried
in winter earth.

For Emma
> *September 25, 2001 - August 21, 2016*

A fledgling robin
hops the woodchipped path,
baby feathers drab camouflage,
belly barely the rusty color
it may become. Its tiny beak
peeps, calls forth a louder "cheep"

from the mother bird, diving in and out
of raised beds, zucchini, zinnias
broccoli, not unlike the Pegasus jets
practicing landings and take-offs
casting shadows over the garden,
filling the air with thunder.

The robin doesn't see her chick,
chirps escalate. I freeze,
bystander to eventual death
if the two don't meet,
possible death even if they do.
Yet minutes ago, I crushed

the yellow larva of bean beetles
their life force pooling on lacelike
leaves, ruined by their eating.
I'm sickened—feel of the squish,
the carcass left behind—
the escalation of my attack.

On this clear blue summer day,
I consider the fledgling, the larva
who will live and who will die.

A Sharp-Shinned Hawk

holds me in thrall,
meets my gaze
as he tears flesh from bird
or rodent, draped
over a backyard branch.

Judge, jury, executioner,
he is Cromwell—in shadows
orange striped vest, gray cloak—
taking the measure
of songbirds and voles.

An invisible chain binds us,
me at the kitchen window—bird books
on the counter, binoculars
no match for his beady eye—
him on his perch, watching me.

A spot of blood soaks his chest,
yellow talons pierce ravaged flesh.
I tell myself I can break the spell
blink, look back
but he has vanished first.

The Pink Dress III

At the edge of the Great Marsh, a house sits
like a spinster, her back straight, her elbows
sharp points, her pink dress worn
so that here and there her silvery
underpinnings start to show through.
Despite aging bones, the paint
peeling from clapboards, she is a Siren,
calling me to sit in the third floor turret
to watch snowy egrets,
their golden-slippered feet
stalking the marsh while
thousands of tree swallows swarm,
wing tip to wing tip
their feathers flashing blue
until the sun darkens and the eel grass
bends under their flight.

Sometimes a White Sheet
after "Untitled" by Ana Teresa Fernandez

flaps, bucks against her body
slaps it, clings to her curves
her fingers press,
pin it to the clothesline.

Long, slim legs crossed,
feet in black stilettos
await her lover
ready to tango, or

tangle in sheets, write
the story of a family—
one flown to heaven
in folds of a shroud—

while the untamed shadow
darkens the grass,
a giant swan dances
with the hidden woman.

Bird Woman
after Danielle Julian Norton

Some days you just want to put on your mask, walk into a different life so you strap on your bird beak and fuzzy wig, don your high-necked long white gown drenched in lace, dip your hands into the closest mud puddle and walk away. Fly the coop. No more cages for you, no more dinosaurs or plastic legos, no nothingness of goulash with leftover meat loaf, no more clip clothespins on sheets outdoors in forty-eight degree weather where you know the bird shit will inevitably land in one small spot, no more fruit flies on the repurposed Tupperware lettuce container-turned-compost bowl, no more craning your neck to look at your sometimes flickering computer monitor or finding yourself lost on twitter instead of actually looking at the birds at the back yard feeders on the pole bent by a marauding bear. Leave that life behind: Soar over empty beaches, take a dust bath in the dirt, rise on the wind currents. Be the raven-crow-hawk-eagle: Dart beak-first at the eyeballs of life.

Birding the Boreal Forest

Our target bird, the black-backed woodpecker
      hides in the fog-laden woods
  just beyond the high tension wires stretched

along Trudeau Road. Like sentinels, we stand
      at the edge of the forest,
  in silence, listening for the rat-a-tat-tat-tat

of the elusive bird. Snow dusts our shoulders,
      our knit toques. Intruders,
  we have seen crossbills, red and white

fed gray jays sunflower seeds. I long to be first
      to spot the black-backed, keep
  my binoculars pressed to my eyes, jump when I hear

the staccato sound of beak on tree, scan right,
      left, up and down: nothing,
  it was our leader playing the call on his iPhone.

He tricked me, but not the bird, who refuses
      to play by our rules,
  to reveal himself to this band of birders.

The call plays again, and again I startle.
      Snow thickens, almost dark
  and I have to concede it's time to leave

though if I could see the black-backed,
      I might stand for one more hour,
  one more hour, just one more hour.

Notes

Language of the Forgotten—The title of this poem is also the title of the first piece I discovered by Titus Kaphar at the Massachusetts Museum of Contemporary Art (MASS MoCA) during a poetry residency in 2018. This particular installation, crafted of charred white oak, high density urethane, glass and LED lights, reveals his goal to investigate the power of a rewritten history. A MacArthur grant winner, he has exhibited his work around the world. https://massmoca.org/event/titus-kaphar/

As If To Explain the World—The Schoolboy of 1850—My first teaching job was at Cushing Academy in Ashburnham, MA where Bela Pratt's statue, *The Schoolboy of 1850* stood at the entrance. Pratt, born in 1867, studied with Augustus St. Gaudens, among others, and launched his career with two colossal sculptural groups for the 1893 World's Columbian Exposition in Chicago. After the Exposition, he began 25 years teaching sculpture at the Boston Museum School and advocating for the role of sculpture in public and private life. https://www.flickr.com/photos/tom22378/4651481974

A Tour of the Archives—Roger Tory Peterson, (August 28, 1908—July 28, 1996) is a world-renowned ornithologist. He is perhaps best known for his illustrated *Field Guide to Birds of North America*, The Roger Tory Peterson Institute, located in Jamestown, New York, houses Peterson's papers, paintings and bird skins among many other artifacts.

An American Visits the Memorial For Twenty Thousand RAF Who Died—On the last day of a trip to England in 2016, the guide wanted us to see the Air Forces Memorial, near Runnymede. This beautiful monument honors 20,456 men and women of the RAF, with no known gravesite, lost during World War II. The memorial was unveiled by Queen Elizabeth in October, 1953. https://www.cwgc.org/visit-us/find-cemeteries-memorials/cemetery-details/109600/runnymede-memorial/

Monumental Inversion—The title of my poem comes from another piece by Titus Kaphar exhibited at MASS MoCA in North Adams, MA. This sculpture, made of wood, hand blown glass and steel, appeared in an exhibit titled *Suffering From Realness*. Kaphar creates the typical heroic pose of George Washington seated on his horse, but it is merely the hollow silhouette carved in a block of wood in which blown glass partially lodges in the body of the horse. Fallen pieces of glass lie on the floor below. https://kapharstudio.com/free-trade/

Blackwater—Sally Mann, a photographer perhaps best known for photographs of her children, has completed a study of the American South where she grew up, and a series of photographs represent the Blackwater rivers and swamps in the region. https://www.getty.edu/art/exhibitions/sally_mann/images/explore/6_371098EX1_x1024.jpg

The Pink Dress II—*Christina's World* by Andrew Wyeth is one of his iconic paintings. My poem grew out of an interview he gave in which he discussed his process and approach in this painting. Though he depicts Christina Olsen in many of his works, I was surprised to learn that she is not the woman in this Maine scene which is so familiar and bears her name in the title. https://www.moma.org/collection/works/78455

What You Wanted—A C-scow is a particular racing sailboat which is "highly maneuverable, furiously fast, and a ton of fun. It has been an intergenerational fixture on the inland lakes for well over 100 years," according to one manufacturer. I never had a ton of fun in the particular C-scow referenced in the poem.

Sometimes a White Sheet—Ana Teresa Fernandez is a versatile artist who works in multiple media on themes of gender and racial equity. She documents her performance art in video and paintings. Her high-heeled shoes are a trademark of her work. My poem is based on the painting at the far left at this link. https://anateresafernandez.com/telarana/

Bird Woman—An enormous photo by Danielle Julian Norton of a woman wearing a bird mask inspired this poem. The photo hung in the lobby of Building 13 at MASS MoCA where visiting artists have studios. Julian Norton is a visual artist working in multi-media installations, as well as video, sculpture, and photography. https://daniellejuliannorton.net/section/270018-Portrait.html

Land Acknowledgment—These poems were written on N'dakinna, the ancestral homeland of the Abenaki, Pennacook and Wabanaki People, past and present. I acknowledge and honor with gratitude the land, waterways and the people who have stewarded the land over the generations.

ACKNOWLEDGMENTS

These poems first appeared in the following journals & anthologies:

The Avocet: "Beasts in the Woods" (as "Jacking Deer")
The Moon: "Post Cards at the New York Historical Society"
museum of americana: "A Tour of the Archives"
The Poeming Pigeon: Poems from the Garden: "For Emma" (as "Elegy for Emma")
Reed Magazine: "Walking to the Bus With My Mother"
Shooter Lit Mag: "Home, Circa 1964," "As If To Explain The World"

In addition I want to acknowledge and thank my fellow writers in Yogurt Poets, based in Concord, NH for their help and feedback over the years and the Boiler House Poets, who have gathered for five years in residence at MASS MoCA in the Assets for Artists Program, for their expert advice and support.

Katherine Morgan is a teacher, gardener, grandmother and social justice activist in the Seacoast Region of New Hampshire. Her prose and poetry have appeared in numerous journals and anthologies. Most recently she was a Co-editor and contributing essayist to *Beyond the Notches: Stories of Place in New Hampshire's North Country* which received the NH Writer's Project award for Outstanding Work of Nonfiction in 2012. The University of Iowa Press published her book *My Ever Dear Daughter, My Own Dear Mother* (1996), a collection of 19th century correspondence between her great, great grandmother and her great grandmother, annotated and introduced by Morgan. She is currently at work on a full length edition of poems and a collection of essays based on an extensive archive of family papers dating back to 1819.

www.ingramcontent.com/pod-product-compliance
Lightning Source LLC
LaVergne TN
LVHW041512070426
835507LV00012B/1503